I0012195

The Digital Nomad's Survival Guide
Work and Travel with Ease

Table of Contents

Chapter 1. Introduction

Welcome adventurer, to the gateway of an exciting journey! Are you yearning for exploration while staying economically active? Eager for adventure, with your work in your backpack? Our Special Report, "The Digital Nomad's Survival Guide: Work and Travel with Ease," is a treasure map. This report not only convinces you that you can comfortably seize the world while working, but it also equips you with tools, tips, and strategies to conquer the challenges. It's your road towards a remarkable, geography-independent career. Before you know it, sandy beaches, lush mountains, or vibrant cities will be your offices. Get ready for the life-altering exploration that awaits! With this special report as your guide, you'll soon be a navigate the digital nomad life, leaving footprints around the globe as you work and travel with ease. See that 'Buy Now' button? Click it! Let's set sail on this extraordinary journey together. Get ready to redefine what a 'day at the office' means to you.

Chapter 2. The Digital Nomad Lifestyle: An Overview

The digital nomad lifestyle is an exciting fusion of work and travel, blending the boundaries between professional commitments and personal enjoyment seamlessly. This modern way of life is invigorating and limitless, offering the thrilling possibility of living and working anywhere globally, as long as there's a stable internet connection available.

2.1. The Birth of Digital Nomadism

In the dawn of the internet era, the traditional concept of work started to shift from a fixed office desk to anywhere a laptop could be opened. Then came digital nomadism—a paradigm shift that transformed the work landscape with its limitless geographical possibilities. Early digital nomads were typically freelancers or entrepreneurs who leveraged the internet's power for remote work while they explored the exciting diversity of the globe—culturally and geographically. The trend has since notably gained momentum, with more professionals choosing the digital nomad path irrespective of their professions and ages.

2.2. The Appeal of the Lifestyle

At the heart of digital nomadism lies an unquenchable thirst for adventure, freedom, and flexibility. One could be working on a high-stakes project with a beach's soothing sounds in the background or taking a conference call while gazing at a serene mountain range. The thrill and charm lie in the power to swap 'office' views at will, while satiating wanderlust and maintaining professional productivity.

But beyond the charm of the beaches, mountains or bustling cities, digital nomadism offers a priceless opportunity to immerse oneself in different cultures, pick new languages, enjoy varied cuisines, and form global networks. It is pretty much a lifestyle that enriches one personally and professionally.

2.3. Working Sectors

Digital nomads come from various sectors—IT, marketing, writing, consulting, design, teaching, and several others. Some are employees who convinced their bosses about effective work-from-home; others are freelancers, entrepreneurs, or digital business owners who operate their firms from anywhere in the world. As technology advances and remote work becomes more accepted, the variety in digital nomads' professions is bound to increase.

2.4. Advantages of Digital Nomadism

While each digital nomad's motivation may be unique, several advantages make this lifestyle increasingly attractive:

1. Flexibility: Digital nomads enjoy unparalleled flexibility—not only in choosing their work hours but also their work location.

2. Adventure: The lifestyle comes bundled with the excitement of traveling, exploring new places, cultures, cuisines, and people.

3. Cost-effective: Living in countries with lower costs of living can offer significant savings.

4. Personal Growth: The mix of professional work and travel leads to immense personal growth and a broader worldview.

5. Networking: Interacting with people worldwide increases one's global network, opening doors to many future prospects.

However, as enchanting as it may sound, digital nomadism undoubtedly comes with its challenges and is not a one-size-fits-all endeavor.

2.5. Challenges

1. Connectivity: While a stable internet connection becomes your lifeline, it isn't always easy or affordable, especially in remote locations or while moving.

2. Time Zone Differences: Working with a team scattered across different time zones can be challenging.

3. Work-Life Balance: Striking a balance between work commitments and explorations can be tough. It's easy to either overlook work or forget to enjoy the location.

4. Legal Issues: Visa regulations, taxation issues, and insurance can be complex and time-consuming.

5. Loneliness: Long-term travel and social disconnect can lead to feelings of loneliness or isolation.

Even with these, with adequate preparedness, one can navigate these challenges smoothly.

2.6. Conclusion

Being a digital nomad isn't just about the glamour of travel or skipping the 9-5 office grind—it's a lifestyle choice that requires careful planning, constant adaptation, and an insatiable yearning for exploration. It's about designing a life that's not bound by geographical constraints but thrives on flexibility, freedom, and growth. As the world remarkably progress towards this radical work model, corporates and governments slowly adjust rules and ensure the ease of operation—perhaps, signaling a future where digital nomadism could become a norm rather than an exception.

While roadblocks exist, they're not insurmountable as evidenced by countless successful digital nomads worldwide. Central to succeeding in this lifestyle is the ability to embrace change, be proactive, remain flexible and, most importantly, keep a backup plan. You are about to step into a world where your 'office' could be anywhere—a remote tropical island, an airy coffee shop, or the comforts of your home.

In the coming chapters, we'll explore in-depth tools, tips, strategies, and practical insights to embark on this exciting voyage and sustain the digital nomad lifestyle with ease. Be it understanding visa regulations, finding reliable health insurance, or selecting the best coworking spaces—this guide will equip you to seize the digital nomad world. It's time you refined what 'a day in the office' means to you. After all, the world is now your workplace, and every day is an adventure.

Chapter 3. Essential Tools for the Modern Wanderer

Kickstarting a location-independent life requires not only a determined mindset and an adventurous spirit but also a set of specific tools. When your office is potentially any place under the sun, the way in which you work and communicate changes drastically. This calls for ample preparation, and that's where this chapter comes in to play. We'll discuss the essential tools for your digital wanderlust journey, thinking in terms of hardware, software, and office requisites.

3.1. Hardware Essentials

The first step in gathering your digital nomad toolset is to invest in reliable hardware. The following list outlines the fundamental components you simply can't afford to compromise on.

- Laptop: As a digital nomad, your laptop is your lifeline. Beyond considering battery life and speed, you might also want to think about weight and size, particularly if you plan to travel often. From MacBooks to Windows-based laptops, choose something that fits your work needs and travel lifestyle.

- Smartphone: A smartphone is a must, serving as your primary means of communication, a tool for accessing essential apps, and potentially even a substitute workstation. An unlocked, dual-SIM smartphone can be especially useful for frequent travellers.

- Backup Drive: Data loss can be devastating. Therefore, always have an external hard drive or a solid-state drive (SSD) to backup vital information. Portable, shock-resistant options are available.

- Universal Adaptor: Power compatibility varies globally. Hence, having a universal adaptor means you won't need to worry about plug variations in different countries.

- Portable Wi-Fi Device: Public Wi-Fi isn't always reliable or secure. For uninterrupted connectivity, consider a portable Wi-Fi hotspot or travel router.

3.2. Software Essentials

With hardware sorted, it's time to focus on the crucial software that will streamline your work-life while on move. Here's what you need:

- Productivity Suite: Depending on your preference, Google Workspace or Microsoft 365 should be your go-to suite for creating and managing documents, spreadsheets, and presentations.

- Communication Tools: Zoom, Slack, or Microsoft Teams facilitate communication with clients or teammates. Choose the ones your contacts are most comfortable with.

- Project Management Tools: Trello, Asana, or JIRA helps in organising tasks, managing projects, and tracking progress.

- Time Management Apps: RescueTime or TimeDoctor can help manage workload and improve productivity. These tools provide a detailed report of your activities, helping you optimise time usage.

- Cloud Storage: Google Drive or Dropbox ensure easy access to your files from anywhere. Not to mention serving as additional backup space.

3.3. Office Requisites

Considerably less tangible than the above categories, the office essentials are all about creating a productive and efficient work environment regardless of your physical location.

- Ergonomic Travel Gear: This can include foldable stands, portable mouse and keyboards, and noise-cancelling headphones. These make a world of difference for comfort and productivity.

- Virtual Mailbox Service: Mail handling can be a challenge while on the move. Services like Earth Class Mail or Anytime Mailbox help manage your mail digitally.

- Co-working Space Membership: Sign up for global co-working space networks like WeWork or Regus, providing you a productive space whenever you need it.

- VPN (Virtual Private Network): This tool keeps your connection secure even in potentially risky public Wi-Fi networks.

- Travel Insurance: Always aim to have comprehensive coverage that includes trip accommodations, health emergencies, and gear protection.

Digital nomadism may appear complex at first glance, but remember: the right preparation smooths out most of the bumps along the way. This exhaustive list is, basically, your survival kit, designed to cater to every need you might have as you boldly venture into your geography-independent career. Take the time to understand what each tool does and gauge its relevance to your specific journey. And remember, each tool is like a compass, guiding you towards successful exploration and productivity. Enjoy the journey, digital wanderer, after all, it's not just about the destination but how you get there!

Chapter 4. Work-Life Balance: Mastering the Art of Flexibility

The digital nomad lifestyle represents a blend of work and life in a way the traditional office job cannot offer. It's a balance of enjoying remarkable places while fulfilling your professional responsibilities. This chapter offers you guidelines to mastering that ever-elusive work-life balance and the art of flexibility on the road.

4.1. Cultivate a Routine: Begin with Structure

Conventional office-based roles often thrive on a structured routine, but as a digital nomad, you may feel that idea crumbles when introduced to the variables of foreign time zones, unfamiliar cultures, and potential Wi-Fi woes. That's where cultivating your routine comes into play.

Creating a personal routine permits you to establish a sense of normalcy, remaining grounded amidst the ever-changing landscape of digital nomadism. Start by setting regular work hours, placing importance on both productivity and time spent outside of work. This might be challenging due to enticing sightseeing opportunities and unexpected travel hiccups, but a steady routine will construct a natural divide between work and personal life.

Set aside regular times for eating meals, exercising, and leisure activities. A morning routine can help start your day on a positive note, while an evening routine can allow proper unwinding before bed. Consider tools like Google Calendar or Habitify to keep track of your routine and maintain consistency.

4.2. Embrace Flexibility and Adaptability

As a digital nomad, unexpected developments are a part of the journey: a last-minute change of Wi-Fi availability, unexpected local holidays, or spontaneous social invitations. Embrace these challenges and encounters as opportunities to flex your adaptability muscle. This is part of the art of the digital nomad lifestyle, where structure meets flexibility and adaptability.

Remember to keep a buffer for work and personal obligations to handle unexpected demands. Adapt your routine as needed, showing flexibility while also respecting your boundaries. It's okay to shuffle things around occasionally to accommodate a can't-miss local festival or an urgent work deadline.

4.3. Manage Your Time Efficiently

Time management is crucial in achieving a healthy work-life balance. Use tools like Asana or Trello for task organization and prioritization. Moreover, remember the Pareto Principle, often referred to as the 80/20 rule - 80% of output is derived from 20% of input. Focusing on key tasks can lead to increased productivity, freeing more time for exploring.

Also, consider the 'time-boxing' technique, where you allocate specific timeframes for different tasks or activities. This promotes focused work periods and helps create a well-rounded daily schedule, including time allocated for work, leisure, socializing, and rest.

4.4. Leverage Technology, but Also Disconnect

Leverage technology to your advantage; it is a critical enabler of the digital nomad lifestyle. Invest in reliable devices, ensure regular data backups, and use collaboration tools for staying connected with teams and clients.

But while technology helps us to stay connected and productive, periodic disconnection is advisable to avoid burnout. Designate 'No Screen Time' in your routine to unwind, explore, and immerse yourself in the local culture without digital distractions. These disconnecting periods can be surprisingly productive for your overall wellbeing and even lead to your most creative ideas.

4.5. Regular Exercise and Healthy Eating

Maintain your health by incorporating regular exercise into your routine, which could range from a quick workout at your accommodation, attending a local fitness class, or simply opting to walk around your destination. Explore local cuisine, but also strive to maintain a balanced diet. These habits contribute to your physical health, which is crucial for sustainable travel and productivity.

4.6. Nurturing Your Mental Well-being

A sense of isolation can sneak up on many digital nomads. Regular interactions with other travelers or digital nomads can minimize this feeling significantly. Engage in social and communal activities, both physically - like local events or co-workspace interactions - and virtually, through online communities.

Meditation and mindfulness practices are beneficial for mental health. Furthermore, staying in touch with family and friends back home, keeping a journal, or engaging in a hobby can contribute positively to your mental well-being.

4.7. Honoring the Digital Nomad Code: Respect Local Communities

A crucial part of the digital nomad lifestyle is respect for the local traditions, customs, and public norms. This not only makes you a responsible traveler, but it also shapes your experiences, knowledge, and stories.

The journey of a digital nomad is indeed filled with thrilling adventures. By mastering the art of flexibility and maintaining a strong work-life balance, you can fully immerse yourself in this lifestyle. The mantra is adapting your routine while staying open to change, leaning on technology but knowing when to disconnect, looking after your health and mental well-being, and honoring the nomad code. By following these guidelines, you'll navigate your digital nomad journey with more ease and joy, making the whole world your office without burning out.

Chapter 5. Traveling Smart: Optimal Destinations for Digital Nomads

The life of a digital nomad often seems idyllic, but choosing the right destination is crucial to successfully balance work with travel. This chapter will guide you through choosing optimal destinations while considering factors like cost of living, quality of life, internet reliability, the digital nomad community, and the overall vibe of the place.

5.1. The Importance of Choosing the Right Destination

Being a digital nomad, your home-office can be anywhere, from a bustling cityscape to a tranquil beach. But choosing the right location is critical. It makes the difference between having a seamless work experience and facing constant challenges. Besides work-friendly infrastructure, other factors like living cost, safety, quality of life, and the existing digital nomad community are equally paramount.

5.2. Factors to Consider While Choosing a Destination

Before picking a destination, a digital nomad should consider the following aspects.

1. Cost of Living: This includes your accommodation, food, transport, and any other expenses you may have.
2. Quality of Internet: A reliable and fast internet connection is vital

for your work.

3. Safety: As you will be living and working abroad, safety should be a top priority.

4. Community: A strong digital nomad community can provide networking opportunities and social interaction.

5. Climate and Culture: These factors add to the overall experience of living and working in a new destination.

5.3. Cost of living

The cost of living is a significant factor for digital nomads who are usually dependent on incomes that might not fluctuate as per the economy of the country they are living in. It is prudent to look for destinations that offer a lifestyle that fits your budget without compromising quality. Countries in South-East Asia, Eastern Europe, and Latin America, for example, are popular for their affordable living costs.

1. South-East Asia: Thailand and Vietnam offer great value for money with cheap accommodations, food, and transportation. Bali in Indonesia is another excellent choice for its inviting beaches and affordable villas.

2. Eastern Europe: Countries like Poland, Romania, and Bulgaria famously offer strong internet combined with lower living costs.

3. Latin America: Mexico, Colombia, and Argentina are known for their low cost of living, and vibrant culture and food scenes.

5.4. Internet Availability

Having a strong and reliable internet connection is non-negotiable for a digital nomad. This factor alone can make or break the deal. It's not just the speed that matters, but also the reliability and cost.

1. Taipei, Taiwan: Renowned for its high-speed internet, it's a technology hub and offers loads of working spaces.

2. Seoul, South Korea: South Korea boasts some of the world's fastest internet speeds and great infrastructure.

3. Northern Europe: Stockholm in Sweden, Helsinki in Finland, and Tallinn in Estonia, all provide blazing fast and reliable internet connectivity.

5.5. Safety

It is critical to check the safety status of the country. Use resources like the Global Peace Index, Travel Advisories from your government, or community feedback from other digital nomads. Also, consider cultural fit, local norms, and respect boundaries while interacting with locals.

1. Iceland: Consistently rated as one of the safest countries in the world. High living costs are offset by the low crime rate and incredible landscapes.

2. Singapore: Famous for its strict orderliness, Singapore is one of the safest cities globally with reliable public transportation.

3. Scandinavia: Denmark, Finland, and Sweden are all highly safe destinations with excellent benefits for its residents.

5.6. Digital Nomad Community

A strong digital nomad community can be a supportive element for those new to the lifestyle. These communities work as social structures, resources for local information, and provide opportunities for collaboration.

1. Chiang Mai, Thailand: Known as the 'Digital Nomad Capital of the World,' Chiang Mai has a large community, coworking spaces,

networking events, and affordable cost of living.

2. Bali, Indonesia: Known for its tropical charm and wellness culture, Bali is a hotspot for digital nomads with numerous coworking spaces and networking opportunities.

3. Medellin, Colombia: It is rapidly growing as a popular spot for digital nomads with its spring-like climate year-round and a fast-growing startup scene.

5.7. Climate and Culture

Choose a destination that fits your preferred climate and cultural interests, contributing to your overall lifestyle and happiness.

1. Canary Islands, Spain: The island offers a pleasant maritime climate year-round, alongside rich Spanish culture and food.

2. Ho Chi Minh City, Vietnam: If tropical climates are your preference, this bustling city with its unique blend of French and Vietnamese culture might be your place.

3. Queenstown, New Zealand: This adventure town is perfect for those wanting a mix of work and an active, outdoor lifestyle.

Make your choices wisely, albeit they aren't fixed. The beauty of being a digital nomad is that you can always pack up and try out a new location if the current one doesn't fit. So, continue exploring, and you'll find your ideal corners of the world to work and live in.

Chapter 6. Tackling Time Zones: Managing Asynchronous Communication

Working remotely provides unmatched freedom to work from anywhere in the world. However, with this freedom comes the challenge of navigating different time zones. This may seem like a daunting task, but with a few strategies and tools, you can manage time zones effectively and achieve seamless asynchronous communication. This chapter will delve into understanding these challenges and provide solutions to tackle them effectively.

6.1. Understanding Asynchronous Communication

First, let's define asynchronous communication. In a traditional office setting, most work is done synchronously. This means you and your colleagues are working at the same time, and discussions or meetings happen instantly. Asynchronous communication, however, is not real-time. Information is sent and received at the convenience of both parties.

The flexibility offered by asynchronous communication is what makes the digital nomad lifestyle possible. It offers freedom to work at your own pace and in your own time frame. But it does demand a different approach and the competence to manage work effectively.

6.2. Challenges of Asynchronous Communication

There are a few challenges you may face when dealing with asynchronous communication in different time zones:

- Delays in communication can lead to slow decision-making processes.

- Collaboration may become complicated because feedback and discussions aren't instantaneous.

- There's an increased risk of misinterpretations or missed information since instant clarifications aren't always possible.

Understanding these challenges is the first step in addressing them and developing solutions.

6.3. Building an Asynchronous Communication Strategy

Having an effective strategy is key to successful asynchronous communication, and should include the following elements:

- Understanding your team's expectations: Make sure everyone knows when they should be working and when they can expect responses.

- Choosing the right tools: This will help manage communication, tasks, and projects.

- Setting clear deadlines: Everyone should know what's expected of them and when.

6.4. Choosing the Right Tools for Asynchronous Communication

There are many digital tools and apps available to assist with coordinating and communicating asynchronously. Some of the most common categories include:

- Communication tools: Options like Slack, Microsoft Teams, and Google Hangouts provide platforms for instant messaging and video calls.

- Project management tools: Tools like Trello, Asana, and Basecamp allow teams to organize and prioritize projects and tasks.

- Time management tools: Tools like World Time Buddy and Every Time Zone can help you keep track of different time zones very efficiently.

Choosing the right tools for your needs and mastering how to use them is critical. These tools streamline digital communications and help align everyone's work.

6.5. Developing Time Zone Awareness

Working across time zones requires a good understanding of those zones and a high level of time zone awareness. Websites and apps can help you understand and track different time zones. Best practices in this area include:

- Always add the time zone when scheduling meetings so it's clear to everyone.

- Use a time converter tool to assist with planning or scheduling.

- Consider the working hours of other team members when

planning tasks and deadlines.

6.6. Encouraging Considerate Communication

Considerate communication refers to respecting everyone's work hours, even though they might be different from yours. Encourage your team to mute notifications during off hours and maintain a balanced work life. Transparent communication about working hours can help foster respect and efficiency among a remote team.

6.7. Juggling Multiple Time Zones

When working with several time zones, you might need to juggle your work schedule to find a common overlapping time. This may mean adjusting your working hours, but ensure that you're not always the one making sacrifices, it should be a team effort. Flexibility is a key characteristic of successful digital nomads.

Effective time zone management and asynchronous communication can be achieved with a combination of understanding, strategy, the right tools, and respect for one's team. While it may seem complex, once conquered, it will become second nature, empowering you to enjoy the benefits of the digital nomad lifestyle.

Chapter 7. Maintaining Robust Health & Fitness on the Move

As you embark on your journey as a digital nomad, one of the key aspects to consider is your health and fitness. The continuous movement, changes in diet, and altered routines may seem to pose challenges to maintaining a healthy lifestyle. However, with the right strategies and deliberate efforts, you will acknowledge that sustaining and even improving your health while globetrotting is not only feasible, but also enjoyable.

7.1. Understand the Importance of Health and Fitness

The first realization for a successful digital nomad life is to know that your health is your true wealth. Remember, without a sound mind and a sound body, your globetrotting experiences will be less joyful and successful. Therefore, take every step with your health considerations at the forefront. Keeping your physical and mental health in check while traveling allows you to perform optimally, offering your best to work and yielding time and energy to explore new places.

7.2. Developing a Healthy Eating Habit

As you move across countries and continents, you will encounter different cuisines, unique delicacies, and of course, the temptation to binge on street food. While it is part of the adventure, deviating too far from a balanced diet can induce health issues.

- Plan your meals: Try to not rely entirely on eating out or grabbing food on the go. Rent accommodations with kitchen facilities and take some time to prepare meals.

- Eat Balanced Meals: Even if the local cuisine is heavy on a specific food group, try to balance it out. Include adequate servings of veggies, proteins, and carbs in your diet.

- Stay Hydrated: Differences in climate and water quality can impact hydration. Keep a sturdy, reusable water bottle handy to stay hydrated throughout the day.

7.3. Maintaining Regular Exercise

Regular physical activity boosts energy, improves mood, and promotes better sleep, contributing to overall wellness. As a digital nomad, you need to adapt to variable resources for working out.

- Make Workouts Fun: Incorporate your workouts into your routine by choosing activities that you enjoy. This could include cycling, hiking, dancing, yoga, or even a quick session of HIIT on the beach.

- Use Fitness Apps: Several workout apps provide comprehensive exercise routines that require minimal or no equipment. These can be followed in the comfort of your accommodation.

- Explore Active Tourism: Try to incorporate activities like walking tours, hiking trails, or renting a bicycle for sightseeing. It's an excellent way to stay active while exploring your surroundings.

7.4. Mental Health is Crucial Too

As thrilling as it can be, the nomadic lifestyle also comes with its share of stress and insecurities. Homesickness, loneliness, or anxiety are not uncommon. Here are a few tips to help maintain your mental equilibrium:

- Stay Connected: Regularly check-in with family and friends back home. The familiarity and emotional connect can help significantly in countering feelings of loneliness or homesickness.

- Meditate: A small daily meditation session significantly helps to keep stress and anxiety at bay.

- Seek Help: If you feel consistently down or anxious, don't hesitate to seek professional help. Several virtual counseling services are available today.

7.5. Adequate Rest and Sleep

Restful sleep is just as crucial as diet and exercise in maintaining health. The hustle of traveling and the pressure to sightsee can sometimes interfere with rest:

- Maintain a Routine: Despite the change in time zones and schedules, try to maintain a consistent sleep schedule.

- Use Sleep Aids: Use aids like sleep masks, earplugs, or white noise machines to ensure your sleep environment is as comfortable as possible.

7.6. Regular Health Check-ups

Don't let your travel and work schedules keep you from regular health check-ups:

- Local Clinics: Avail services of local clinics for regular health check-ups. It helps catch any potential issues early.

- Telemedicine: If visiting a local clinic seems challenging, consider telehealth services for routine check-ups and minor health concerns.

In conclusion, being a digital nomad doesn't mean compromising your well-being. It means adapting to new environments and incorporating health management into your adventurous lifestyle. With these strategies in your toolbox, you'll be well equipped to maintain a dynamic balance of work, travel, and health. So go on, take the leap and embrace the road ahead, knowing your wellness strategies are in place.

Chapter 8. Financial Management: Budgeting and Saving Strategies

Navigating the world as a digital nomad offers the thrilling ability to combine work and travel, but doing so requires a keen eye on the financials of things. Successfully managing your budget and savings will be instrumental in having a smooth journey.

8.1. Understanding Your Expenses

Before devising a budget plan, it's critical to understand your expenses. Note down every detail of your expenditures, including rent, food, transportation, utilities, insurance, and unexpected costs that often crop up when traveling.

To help you begin, here's a simple list for you to consider:

- Lodging
- Groceries/Food
- Transportation
- Health/Travel Insurance
- Phone/Internet
- Leisure/Entertainment
- Co-work space fees

Take your time to research the cost of living in your chosen destinations and make adjustments accordingly to accommodate fluctuations in currency value or inflation.

Keep an eye on the exchange rates as well; getting a good

understanding of the rates can help you avoid unexpected high costs when you least expect them.

8.2. Creating a Robust Budget Plan

Now that you've identified your expenses, it's time to develop a solid budget plan. Start by first determining your income. As a digital nomad, this might not always remain constant, so come up with an average earning metric for your plan.

Next, categorize your expenses into fixed and variable outlays. Fixed expenses include those you'll pay regardless of your location, such as insurance, student loans, or cloud storage subscriptions. On the other hand, variable costs are those that will differ based on your location such as groceries, accommodation, and local commuting.

Allocate your income among these categories, making sure to cover the important aspects first. Remember to always set aside funds for an emergency. This humble beginning can later be compounded into your savings.

8.3. Harnessing the Power of Useful Tools

Thankfully, you don't have to manage finances manually. An array of tools and applications are available to assist in budgeting.

Tools like Mint, You Need a Budget (YNAB), and Expensify can provide powerful insights into your spending pattern and help manage your finances effortlessly. Likewise, apps like TransferWise for currency conversion and international fund transfers, and Splitwise for splitting bills can make financial management a breeze.

Leverage these tools, keep track of your transactions, and in no time, you'll become a pro at managing your finances.

8.4. Savings: Building Your Safety Cushion

As a digital nomad, it's tempting to spend on experiences. However, maintaining a healthy financial foundation means you must allocate a certain percentage of your income to savings. This will serve as your safety net, helping you confront any unforeseen issues.

Start saving little by little until it becomes a habit. Reward yourself occasionally but make sure it doesn't dig a hole into your savings. Automate your savings if you find it hard to discipline yourself.

Check for high-yield savings account options where you can grow your money. Do your research and open an account that serves your interests best.

8.5. Managing Taxes

Tax planning and understanding can be quite a challenge for the digital nomad. You're responsible for knowing the tax implications in your home country and the country you're currently residing in.

Ensure that you're clear about your tax status, and don't hesitate to consult with a tax professional if things get confusing. Tools like TurboTax can help simplify your tax process, but a professional can provide more personalized advice.

8.6. Consideration for Long-Term Goals

Balancing your present lifestyle and planning for your future is crucial. This includes things like retirement planning, property investments, or any large-scale project you are thinking about.

Apps like Betterment or Vanguard can be helpful for retirement planning even while you're moving around the world. These platforms can also be used for investment purposes to grow your wealth.

8.7. Enjoying Economical Travel

Being a successful digital nomad also means becoming an economical traveler. Prioritize traveling during the off-season, staying at affordable accommodations, and taking advantage of points and miles for flights.

To add, using rideshares, cooking your own meals instead of always dining out, discovering local, cheaper entertainment options over pricey tourist traps will go a long way in keeping your travel costs down while still ensuring a rich experience.

Financial management as a digital nomad is not just about survival, but blossoming in an exciting lifestyle without unnecessary stress. A well-defined, robust financial strategy is your golden ticket to a successful nomadic lifestyle. So, strategize, budget, save, and explore the world while staying economically active and secure. Never let money problems hinder your nomad spirit!

Chapter 9. Local Cultures: Adapting, Respecting, and Learning

Stepping off the plane into a foreign landscape is much like diving headfirst into a body of water. You're both immersed and surrounded by something entirely different from your normal environment. Becoming a digital nomad means a commitment to continuous adaptation, not just in terms of time zones and work schedules, but also to varying cultures and lifestyle norms. Cultures across the globe are as diverse as the colors in a rainbow—each one unique and vibrant in its own way.

9.1. Embracing Cultural Diversity

Every culture carries with it a fascinating palette of myths, customs, social norms, etiquette, and perceptions. Being culturally sensitive is all about embracing this diversity, beyond observing it from a distance. It's about gaining awareness and promoting a positive mindset towards the differences and similarities we share with others.

Respect is fundamental in this equation. It's more than refraining from making offensive remarks or mocking cultural features. It's about countering stereotypes, appreciating cultural uniqueness, not imposing our own cultural norms onto others, and acknowledging that our ways are not superior.

So how does one gain cultural competency while being on the road, hopping from one country to another?

9.2. Learning Through Observation and Interaction

The first step towards cultural adaptation lies in observation. Pay attention to the locals, how they interact with each other and their surroundings. Notice their communication style, body language, manners, daily habits, and workflow. Indeed, everyone won't fit into a single mold, but you can glean general patterns and unwritten societal rules.

Interactions also pave the way for cultural learning. Strike conversations with locals—the taxi driver, the neighborhood store owner, the person sitting next to you at a café. Try learning a few key phrases in the local language. Frequency and depth of interactions can vary, but each exchange offers a chance to understand their perspectives and ways.

9.3. Understanding Cultural Nuances and Etiquettes

Every culture has its specific codes of conduct and social etiquette. In Japan, for instance, it's common to bow as a form of greeting, while in New Zealand, it could be the pressing of noses (Hongi). Giving or receiving items with the right hand is considered respectful in India, while in Greece, it's considered rude to show the palm of your hand. Knowing these little cultural edicts helps in avoiding misunderstandings and conveying respect for their customs.

9.4. Researching and Reading

Before setting foot in a new location, make a habit of conducting thorough research about its culture, lifestyle, and norms. Books, documentaries, travel blogs, local websites, podcasts can offer insightful perspectives. Many cities have cultural training or language workshops that you can attend. This pre-journey research helps layer your observations and interactions on the ground.

9.5. Participating in Local Culture

Involvement in community events, festivals, public meetings is a great way to learn about a culture. Understanding the significance of a temple festival or the history behind a dance form not only informs you about the particular culture's richness but also triggers mutual sharing and learning.

9.6. Adapting and Reporting Respectfully

Our understanding and engagement with a culture refine our way of reporting about it. If you're a blogger, podcaster, or social media enthusiast posting your experiences, be conscious of how you represent them. Avoid sweeping generalizations, stereotype reinforcements, or negative comparison. Share your experiences as they were—learning experiences.

9.7. Networking with Fellow Nomads

In any given location, there will likely be fellow digital nomads. Exchange notes with them. Their experiences can offer invaluable tips regarding local customs, popular norms, or faux pas to avoid. Informal gatherings, coworking spaces, or online forums offer perfect platforms for such exchanges.

9.8. Practice Religious and Political Sensitivity

Approach religious beliefs, political views, and regional conflicts with sensitivity. Avoid provocative discussions, offensive comments, or inappropriate actions. Being respectful towards sensitive matters proves that you genuinely value their culture.

9.9. Asking When in Doubt

It's normal to feel unsure at times when every street corner holds the possibility of a cultural faux pas. When in doubt, ask. Locals appreciate genuine interest and willingness to learn.

In this era of constant connectivity, adapting to the local culture isn't just about survival. It's about enriching your global nomadic journey, establishing connections, and building bridges of understanding. It's about growing personally and professionally as you surf different cultural waves. Remember, every culture you encounter has something to offer, and every interaction presents an opportunity to learn. Feasting on delicacy, logging into work from an exotic beach, chatting with a fellow nomad, each experience belies a process of transformation. You become a citizen of the world, defying geographical boundaries, and cultivating a multicultural lens to perceive the world around.

Chapter 10. Dealing with Isolation and Building a Nomadic Community

The nomadic journey, with all its allure, magic, and adventure, isn't devoid of challenges. Undeniably, one of the prime hurdles digital nomads often face is isolation. It's an unavoidable reality for those who continue to move from one place to another, leaving behind familiar faces and places. Luckily, the modern world has brought a great deal of flexibility and solutions, in this case, to help you overcome isolation and build a thriving community of your virtual tribe.

10.1. Understanding the Challenge of Isolation

Between ticking off new places from your bucket list and meeting work deadlines, you inevitably immerse yourself in a unique lifestyle. However, this continuous uprooting can also lead to bouts of loneliness and isolation. With each new destination, the bubble of familiarity bursts, and you are left to rebuild your social circle.

Feeling isolated can be intense, especially when you are in a different time zone, away from your home, friends, and family. Dealing with these transient phases of loneliness and maintaining mental well-being are undeniably crucial for digital nomads. Understanding this necessity is the first and essential step in handling isolation and strategizing ways to connect with others.

10.2. Building a Nomadic Community: An Antidote to Loneliness

Creating a sense of community, especially one that understands and mirrors your lifestyle, can significantly help deal with the feeling of isolation. Here's your guide on how to build a nomadic community:

Online Platforms and Local Meetups: There's an abundance of online platforms and local meetups dedicated to digital nomads. Websites like Meetup, Eventbrite, or Facebook Groups can connect you with people living a similar lifestyle. The proximity can help foster close-knit relationships. These platforms are particularly useful when you move to a new city.

Co-Living and Co-Working Spaces: With the rise of remote work, co-living and co-working spaces have been sprouting all over the world. Embarking on a co-living experience ensures that you are constantly around like-minded individuals. Co-working spaces provide an office-like environment where you can not only focus on your work but also meet other digital nomads.

Networking Events and Conferences: Various networking events and conferences offer a platform to connect with a community of remote workers, often leading to lifelong friendships and collaborations.

In the following sections, we will delve deeper into these tactics, providing practical information and resources, helping you to build your nomadic community.

10.3. Harnessing the Power of Online Platforms and Local Meetups

Online platforms and meetups can be an excellent resource for digital nomads. Not only do they make networking easier, but they can also provide useful information about your new city. Here's a step-by-step guide on how to use these platforms:

1. Join a Platform: The first step is to find and join an appropriate platform. Websites like Meetup.com or Eventbrite.com are particularly useful for finding local events or meetups.

2. Research and Attend Relevant Events: Once you've joined a platform, it's time to explore. Find local events, webinars, or meetups that align with your interests and needs. You might just make lifelong professional contacts or friends in these gatherings.

3. Actively Participate: Go the extra mile by participating in discussions, panels, and social activities. Chime in with your inputs and share your personal experiences of being a digital nomad.

Remember, the key to a successful meetup experience is consistent participation and engagement.

10.4. Making the Most of Co-Living and Co-Working Spaces

Co-living and co-working spaces are havens for digital nomads. They foster a sense of community and encourage collaboration. Here are some tips on how to make the most of these spaces:

Location is Key: Choose a co-working space near your living area. This will not only save you commuting time but also increase the chances of networking with people in your vicinity.

Participation is Crucial: Attend the events hosted by these spaces. They often organize workshops, seminars, and networking events.

Share and Learn: Leverage the talent and knowledge of the community. Co-working spaces thrive on collaboration. Learn from your co-workers and share your skills as well.

10.5. Maximizing Networking Events and Conferences

Networking events and conferences are often filled with people who share the same values and live a similar lifestyle. To get the most out of them, follow these strategies:

Plan Ahead: Research about upcoming events and conferences in your current city or future destinations. Plan your schedule accordingly.

Don't Shy Away: Networking events are all about meeting new people. Don't hold back from striking a conversation, sharing your experiences, or exchanging contacts for future opportunities.

Follow Up: Once the event is over, make sure you follow up with the people you've met. It's an excellent way to keep the communication going and strengthen the relationship.

Above all, remember, everyone faces isolation when they break their bubbles of comfort. What matters is how you tackle it. In a world where geographical barriers are fading away, a solid nomadic community can make you feel at home, no matter where you are.

Chapter 11. Emergency Situations: Risks, Preparation, and Mitigation

Living a digital nomad lifestyle is an incredible adventure, but it's not without its challenges, especially when it comes to dealing with emergency situations. The truth is, emergencies can happen anywhere, anytime. As a digital nomad, you may be more exposed to certain risks due to unfamiliar environments and potential language barriers. The key to overcoming these challenges lies in effective preparation and mitigation strategies.

11.1. Understanding the Risks

A comprehensive understanding of the potential risks is paramount. From health crises to natural disasters, digital nomads can face a variety of emergencies. An acute awareness of these potential dangers not only allows you to take precautionary measures but also prepares you mentally to handle them effectively.

11.1.1. Health Emergencies

Living in unfamiliar surroundings means being exposed to different types of illnesses. Food poisoning, infections, or injuries are common examples of such complications. It is crucial to be informed about health risks specific to the region you're venturing into.

11.1.2. Natural Disasters

Earthquakes, tsunamis, floods, or even forest fires are natural calamities that can occur without warning. It's crucial to understand the geographic risks associated with your destination.

11.1.3. Personal Security

All places come with their unique security situations. Petty crimes, scams, terror attacks, or political unrest may pose a danger depending on the destination. Researching about safety in the locale is a must.

11.1.4. Data Security

Being a digital nomad means often relying on public Wi-Fi, which can make you vulnerable to data theft. Protecting your confidential data from local cyber threats is another aspect you need to be aware of.

11.2. Preparation is Key

Proper preparation can be the difference between a minor inconvenience and a major catastrophe. Here are some steps you can take.

11.2.1. Local Laws and Customs

Knowledge of local laws and customs is a must. It helps avoid unnecessary legal conflicts and also fosters a respectful relationship with the local culture.

11.2.2. Health Insurance

Invest in a good health insurance policy covering global health emergencies, accidents, and routine healthcare. Also, consider getting coverage for evacuation in case of severe health emergencies.

11.2.3. Emergency Savings

Set aside savings to cover a substantial period of non-income. This can be used in case of emergencies or any unexpected developments.

11.2.4. Travel Advisories

Always check the travel advisories issued by your home country's foreign affairs department. They provide valuable information about the safety, health risks, and political situation of a place.

11.2.5. Data Protection

Secure your data using VPNs (Virtual Private Networks), secure your system with robust firewalls and antivirus software, and also ensure regular backing up of your data.

11.3. Mitigation Strategies

Despite all precautions, emergencies might occur. In such situations, the ability to mitigate the effects becomes critical.

11.3.1. Panic is Your Biggest Enemy

Keeping calm firstly allows you to think with a clear mind. This could be the difference between making a sound decision or a disastrous one.

11.3.2. Use Your Resources

Use your insurance, contact your embassy, or reach out to friends and family for help whenever required.

11.3.3. Compile Emergency Contacts beforehand

Compiling a list of emergency contacts for each location and keeping it accessible can save valuable time in crisis situations.

11.3.4. Build a Local Support Network

A local support network will give you insights on safety, provide immediate help, and can even become your emergency contacts.

Navigating the digital nomad life requires adroitness. However, with the right understanding, preparation, and the capability to mitigate, you can confidently stride into this exhilarating life, knowing you're capable of handling any emergency situations that may come your way. Your journey into the digital nomad life can then carry on with minimal disruption, even amidst unexpected events.

www.ingramcontent.com/pod-product-compliance
Lightning Source LLC
LaVergne TN
LVHW051627050326
832903LV00033B/4691